TO THE WOMAN
THANK YOU FOR BEING MINE

To the Woman I Love,

THANK YOU FOR
BEING MINE

Scott Matthews
Tamara Nikuradse

FAWCETT COLUMBINE / NEW YORK

A Fawcett Columbine Book
Published by Ballantine Books

Copyright © 1994 by Scott Matthews and Tamara Nikuradse

All rights reserved under International and Pan-American Copyright Conventions. Published in the United States by Ballantine Books, a division of Random House, Inc., New York, and simultaneously in Canada by Random House of Canada Limited, Toronto.

Library of Congress Catalog Card Number: 93-90740

ISBN: 0-449-90915-8

Cover design by Richard Hasselberger
Text design by Mary A. Wirth

Manufactured in the United States of America
First Edition: February 1994

10 9 8 7 6 5 4

Dedicated to all women,
who make these thank-yous possible.

ACKNOWLEDGMENTS

*W*e'd like to thank the following couples who have been great role models for us over the years: Glenn and Gail Matthews, Brett Matthews and Ginger Salazar-Matthews, Lynne and Jim Salmon, Bruce and Gingee Thunberg, Gap and Gram Matthews, Gram Thunberg and Leo McClosky, Tanya Townes and Tim Moynihan, Alexander Nikuradse and Turbo Utta, and Charles and Odeline Townes.

Thank you to all of the people at Ballantine who brought this book to you, especially Matthew Shear and our editor, Sherri Rifkin, for their tremendous efforts. And finally, a special thank-you to Barbara Alpert and Mary Jane Ross for all their help and encouragement.

INTRODUCTION

*I*n keeping with the spirit of our two previous books—*Dear Mom, Thank You for Being Mine* and *Dear Dad, Thank You for Being Mine*—we wanted to thank one another for the love, support, understanding, and for all the many things that we have given to each other during our twelve years together. This book is inspired by those twelve years.

We hope the following thank-yous spark special memories for you and inspire you to write your own thank-yous to the woman you love. Your words and expressions of love will make this collection even more meaningful. Feel free to cross out words and personalize the thank-yous or enter your special thank-yous on the blank page at the end of the book. If some of the thank-yous written in this book do not apply to your love, and you want them to, why not drop the hint and write *(HINT . . . HINT . . .)* or *NOT!!!* after our thank-you.

We wish you lots of love, happiness, and serendipity.

Scott and Tamara

To the Woman I Love,

Thank you for being
my love at first sight.

Thank you for not telling me to "get lost"
when I asked you for a date.

*T*hank you for a great first date
from start to finish.

*T*hank you for returning my call
after the first date.

*T*hank you for that first kiss,
which will last a lifetime.

*T*hank you for making my dreams come true
by going out on a second date with me.

*T*hank you for giving your old beaus pink slips when a fortune-teller told you a handsome, intelligent, worldly, aristocratic gentleman with a great personality and rippling biceps would sweep you off your feet.

*T*hank you for letting me be that gentleman.

*T*hank you for promoting me from friend to boyfriend and letting me call you "babe."

*T*hank you for showing up at my office door at lunchtime with a picnic basket.

*T*hank you for winning a huge stuffed animal for me at the county fair.

*T*hank you for treating me to an espresso at a sidewalk café after a Saturday night movie.

*T*hank you for making goofy faces with me in a dime-store photo booth.

*T*hank you for riding with me on a merry-go-round.

*T*hank you for taking me on an elephant ride at the "Greatest Show on Earth."

*T*hank you for overcoming your butterflies and singing "My Guy" to me in front of a roomful of strangers at a karaoke bar.

*T*hank you for seeing a horror film with me and grabbing my arm at the scary parts.

*T*hank you for not being
a "fatal attraction."

$\mathcal{T}$hank you for taking me
on a horse-and-buggy ride.

$\mathcal{T}$hank you for meeting me in the middle
when we both started chewing at different ends
of the same licorice stick.

*T*hank you for taking me to my
favorite Chinese restaurant and
insisting on paying the bill.

*T*hank you for knocking me off my feet
when you said, "I love you."

$\mathcal{T}$hank you for spraying your 20-page, single-spaced love letters with perfume and stamping them with lipstick kisses.

$\mathcal{T}$hank you for storing my love letters to you in a safe and secure place where no one will ever find them.

*T*hank you for tying cans to the back of my car and taping a "Just in Love!" sign on the trunk.

*T*hank you for sitting with me in the front seat of a roller coaster and screaming like a maniac with your arms in the air.

*T*hank you for being my not-so-secret admirer.

$\mathcal{T}$hank you for playing the combination of our birthdays in the lottery in the hope of escaping to some tropical island in the South Pacific, far from the madding crowd, where we can sip margaritas while lounging on beach chaises.

$\mathcal{T}$hank you for believing me when I tell you I've already won the jackpot because I have you, and the annuity pays out over a lifetime.

*T*hank you for faxing love poems to me
that promise a wonderful life together.

*T*hank you for holding
my hand during doubleheaders.

*T*hank you for not getting too jealous
when there's a message on my answering
machine from an old girlfriend.

*T*hank you for telling me to go fly a kite—
and then flying one with me in the park.

*T*hank you for leaving behind Hershey's Kisses
when you couldn't be there to kiss me in person.

*T*hank you for not entering our relationship
with preconceived notions or a rule book.

*T*hank you for calling me every night before
you went to sleep just to say "good night."

*T*hank you for placing a newspaper
ad declaring your love for me.

*T*hank you for holding me close
during our moonlight strolls.

$\mathscr{T}$hank you for practicing safe sex
before you met me.

$\mathscr{T}$hank you for waiting until
I was ready to go all the way.

$\mathscr{T}$hank you for making our "first time" making
love the most incredible, indelible, edible,
delectable, and unforgettable experience ever!

$\mathcal{T}$hank you for waking up with a smile on your face instead of pretending that the night before didn't happen and running out the door.

$\mathcal{T}$hank you for respecting me in the morning.

$\mathcal{T}$hank you for feeling comfortable enough with me to let me see you without your makeup on.

*T*hank you for finally giving me
a key to your place and my *very own*
corner to throw my clothes in.

*T*hank you for wanting to meet my parents.

*T*hank you for impressing my family with your grace, wit, charm, and intelligence.

*T*hank you for complimenting my parents without making it *too* obvious.

*T*hank you for sneaking into my bedroom for a little hanky-panky in the middle of the night when we stayed at my parents' house.

*T*hank you for not getting caught.

*T*hank you for warning me what
to say and what not to say
to your parents before our
first meeting.

*T*hank you for bringing me to
a family reunion and not abandoning me
with your talkative Uncle Herb.

$\mathcal{T}$hank you for stopping at a busy playground
and dreaming of a day when we have children
who will make this world a brighter place.

$\mathcal{T}$hank you for booking us into a deluxe
hotel around the corner from where
you live for a luxurious night.

*T*hank you for walking barefoot on a deserted beach with me during the off season.

*T*hank you for spending a rainy fall afternoon with me in an art museum.

*T*hank you for being my homecoming date and a good sport as you sat on the cold, wet bleachers during the football game.

*T*hank you for dressing up with me as
Romeo and Juliet on Halloween.

*T*hank you for rolling with me in a pile
of leaves and letting me be on top.

*T*hank you for picking a bushel of apples
and baking an apple pie with me.

*T*hank you for making hay with me on
the back of a wagon during a hayride.

*T*hank you for cooking a scrumptious
Thanksgiving feast with me for my relatives.

*T*hank you for calling my favorite radio
station to have *our* song dedicated
to me during my morning drive.

$\mathcal{T}$hank you for hiding love notes in my
suit pocket, my wallet, and my car.

$\mathcal{T}$hank you for sparing me the fun and
adventure of baby showers and cat shows.

$\mathcal{T}$hank you for playing footsie with me under
my parents' table during dinner parties.

*T*hank you for setting the timer on the camera so we'd have a picture of us.

*T*hank you for doodling hearts around our initials.

*T*hank you for wearing strapless dresses that accentuate your cleavage.

$\mathcal{T}$hank you for giving me a
"pettifore" by clipping my toenails.

$\mathcal{T}$hank you for playing hooky from work
with me and going to a musical matinee.

$\mathcal{T}$hank you for feeding
me frozen grapes in bed.

*T*hank you for watching "Frosty the Snowman,"
"The Grinch Who Stole Christmas," "Rudolph
the Red Nosed Reindeer," and "Santa Claus Is
Coming to Town" year after year after year.

*T*hank you for braving the Christmas crowds
to shop with me up to the last minute.

*T*hank you for licking the Christmas card envelopes and stamps, all 101 of them.

*T*hank you for making shopping for your gifts an easy expedition by dropping discreet hints (like drawing big red circles around certain items in catalogs and marking the circles with exclamation points).

*T*hank you for teaching me how to wrap
gifts properly so they don't look like something
that goes out with the trash.

*T*hank you for kissing me
whenever we stand under mistletoe.

*T*hank you for not baking
fruitcakes for my relatives.

*T*hank you for putting up with my protests
when I didn't want to go to *The Nutcracker*
for the second year in a row.

*T*hank you for not being a nutcracker.

*T*hank you for being my secret Santa and
not stuffing my stocking with coal.

*T*hank you for celebrating our very own
Christmas before we visited our relatives.

*T*hank you for kissing me at midnight
and making shared promises with me for
our New Year together.

Thank you for not breaking too many
of your New Year's resolutions
by the second week in January.

Thank you for throwing the first
snowball to start a snowball fight.

Thank you for building a snowman in the
park and letting me decapitate it before
the neighborhood kids got the pleasure.

*T*hank you for pulling off my winter boots
and rubbing the blood back into my
freezing toes after a romp in the snow.

*T*hank you for making me hot cocoa with those
little marshmallows on a cold winter's eve.

*T*hank you for chasing away my winter
blues with your warm smiles.

$\mathcal{T}$hank you for buying salty snacks and beer and throwing a Super Bowl party for the two of us so that we could cheer on our team. (Go Bills!)

$\mathcal{T}$hank you for sharing your erotic dreams that included me and keeping quiet about those other dreams that didn't include me.

*T*hank you for removing
the lint from my belly button.

*T*hank you for blowing
sloppy kisses on my belly.

*T*hank you for attending an RV show with me
and dreaming about our retirement, when we can
spend every day together driving along Route 66.

*T*hank you for doing the little things that
make me happy just because.

*T*hank you for not
plastering your face with makeup.

*T*hank you for declaring a "Honey
Appreciation Day" and honoring me all day.

*T*hank you for scrubbing my back
in the shower with a loofah pad.

*T*hank you for explaining
what a loofah is.

$\mathcal{T}$hank you for saying "YES!" when I popped the big question and saving me from a life of bachelorhood.

$\mathcal{T}$hank you for acting surprised even though you expected the ring all along despite my best intentions to fake you out.

*T*hank you for understanding that the size
of the diamond on your engagement ring
does not measure my love for you.

*T*hank you for crying tears of happiness when it
finally dawned on you that you'd be marrying me.

*T*hank you for warning me about your father's
plan to interrogate me about my intentions.

*T*hank you for preparing a Valentine's Day dinner of oysters and green M&Ms for dessert.

*T*hank you for being in the direct path of my Cupid's arrow.

*T*hank you for not checking us into a cheesy motel with mirrors on the ceiling and a vibrating bed that takes quarters as a Valentine's Day surprise.

*T*hank you for being my genie and granting
me three wishes.

*T*hank you for granting my first wish when you
said you would marry me.

*T*hank you for granting my second wish when
you said you'd spend the rest of your life with me.

*T*hank you for granting my third wish when
you said you'd be the mother of our children.

*T*hank you for holding my hand
in public no matter how sweaty it got.

*T*hank you for taking massage classes and
demonstrating the ancient techniques on me.

*T*hank you for building
a photo shrine of me in your office.

*T*hank you for celebrating
the anniversary of our first kiss.

*T*hank you for always fooling me on April 1, like
the time you applied a temporary tattoo
on your shoulder that read "DADDY."

*T*hank you for helping (and making)
me meet my deadlines every April 15.

$\mathcal{T}$hank you for exchanging
"I" for "we."

$\mathcal{T}$hank you for taking me for a ride on a bicycle built for two and pedaling most of the way uphill.

$\mathcal{T}$hank you for going to a Little League ball game, even when we don't know any of the players, so that I can relive the memories of the ball going through my legs.

*T*hank you for leaving
sexy messages on my voice mail.

*T*hank you for mourning with me
the loss of yet another hair to my brush.

*T*hank you for finding the
best seats at the theater-in-the-park.

$\mathcal{T}$hank you for being my
very own Victoria's Secret model.

$\mathcal{T}$hank you for putting a little more emphasis in
your derrière when you walk away from me.

$\mathcal{T}$hank you for being my pillow.

$\mathcal{T}$hank you for not talking to your plants
more than you talk to me.

*T*hank you for writing "I love you"
in the steam on the bathroom mirror.

*T*hank you for being the sexiest woman alive.

*T*hank you for putting
together photo scrapbooks so that we can
revisit all of our great times.

$\mathcal{T}$hank you for snuggling with me under
a quilt when I'm not feeling well.

$\mathcal{T}$hank you for writing a fan letter
telling me why you're my biggest fan.

$\mathcal{T}$hank you for sending a card to my mother on
Mother's Day thanking her for creating me.

$\mathcal{T}$hank you for pitching a tent
in the backyard and camping out.

$\mathcal{T}$hank you for renting a room
at a spa and hot-tubbing with me.

$\mathcal{T}$hank you for surprising me with plane tickets
to a secret destination known only to you.

*T*hank you for packing my
swim trunks, kidnapping me, and
taking me to a water amusement park.

*T*hank you for making love to me on a
secluded beach and cooling off with a skinny-dip.

*T*hank you for lying with me in an open
field of cool grass on a summer night,
wishing upon a shooting star, and discussing
how we were lovers in a prior lifetime.

*T*hank you for writing "I love you" in the air with
sparklers on the Fourth of July.

*T*hank you for not getting too mad when I threw
you in a pool or put an ice cube down your back.

$\mathcal{T}$hank you for building sand castles with me.

$\mathcal{T}$hank you for kicking the surf with me during a
long walk on the beach.

$\mathcal{T}$hank you for protecting me from those deadly
UV rays by rubbing SPF 15 sun screen all
over me (including my scalp).

*T*hank you for relinquishing control of the barbecue to me, "King Potentate of All Barbecues, Master of All Grills."

*T*hank you for wearing
short shorts on hot days.

*T*hank you for shaving your legs, underarms, and
the borders of your bikini line regularly.

*T*hank you for cleaning
my razor after you shave.

*T*hank you for exploring
mountain trails on long hikes.

*T*hank you for learning to say "I love you"
in seven foreign languages.

*T*hank you for not emasculating me with
pruning shears when I gave you cause.

*T*hank you for creating love coupons
to be redeemed for chores or fun favors.

*T*hank you for not ruining my shirts
with lipstick smudges on my collars.

*T*hank you for licking off my milk mustache.

*T*hank you for finding out-of-the-way
jazz bars with good bands.

*T*hank you for finding the perfect perch
for gazing at a sunset with me.

$\mathcal{T}$hank you for intoxicating me
with the elixir of your love.

*T*hank you for loving me
more than you love your cat.

*T*hank you for understanding that when my dog
Woofums growls at you it is just jealousy.

*T*hank you for growing to tolerate
Woofums even though he slobbers all over you
as a sign of his affection.

*T*hank you for letting Woofums take up one
half of the couch and me the other half.

*T*hank you for not making me explain
why Woofums chases his tail.

*T*hank you for not hitting Woofums every time
he sniffs your most intimate of areas. (Bad dog.)

*T*hank you for not hurting Woofums'
feelings by calling him a stupid mutt.

*T*hank you for staying up late
to watch "Saturday Night Live" reruns
from the days of Belushi and Radner.

*T*hank you for taking me to movies
on sneak preview nights and buying
a large bucket of popcorn to share.

$\mathcal{T}$hank you for recording your thoughts
of love and slipping the tape in my car cassette
player as an early morning pick-me-up.

*T*hank you for not expecting me to go on your
I-Have-to-Lose-10-More-Pounds-to-Fit-into-My-
Wedding-Dress
Diet with you.

*T*hank you for not making me eat rice
cakes and carrot sticks when I was in the
mood for potato chips and ice cream.

*T*hank you for fixing up some of
my friends with your girlfriends.

*T*hank you for not holding it against me for too
long when my friends said your girlfriends were air-
heads with only one thing on their minds.

*T*hank you for vowing never
to fix up our friends again.

*T*hank you for fulfilling my rock-and-roll
teen fantasy 18 years later by taking me
to an Aerosmith concert.

*T*hank you for browsing in bookstores with me.

*T*hank you for coloring
your roots when they grow out.

$\mathscr{T}$hank you for not canceling the wedding
after the 1,293 fights over the smallest details,
like the right shade of white for the wedding
invitations, having tails or no tails for
the groomsmen, whether or not to seat my
single aunt at the table with the most eligible
bachelors, your mother's involvement . . .

*T*hank you for agreeing to register
at my favorite store, The Sharper Image.

*T*hank you for getting all of that
great loot at your wedding showers.

*T*hank you for paring down your invitation list
from 512, even though it meant your second
cousin's butcher's wife was left off the list.

*T*hank you for not making me
sign a prenuptial agreement.

*T*hank you for swearing to me that
you didn't stuff dollar bills down the pants
of some sweaty Chippendale's dancer
during your bachelorette party.

*T*hank you for not losing your cool 24 hours
before the ceremony when my mom told you that I
was allergic to lilies of the valley, the flowers
in your bouquet. *Ah . . . Ah . . . Choo!*

*T*hank you for not making
your cat your maid of honor.

*T*hank you for being the most beautiful
bride ever to walk down the aisle.

*T*hank you for not forgetting
your lines . . . *I do.*

*T*hank you for vowing
to love, honor, and cherish me.

*T*hank you for crying
tears of joy during the ceremony.

*T*hank you for making an
honest man out of me!

*T*hank you for throwing your
bouquet in the direction of my aunt.

*T*hank you for not *mooshing* the wedding cake all
over my face during the cake-cutting ceremony.

*T*hank you for insisting that our guests
throw birdseed instead of rice so that
the birds could celebrate too.

*T*hank you for making our wedding day
the happiest day of my life.

*T*hank you for writing my share
of the thank-you notes that I
promised to write three months ago.

*T*hank you for our spare-no-expense,
run-up-the-debt, all-night-romps-in-the-bed
honeymoon.

*T*hank you for grinning from ear to ear
when you close your eyes and
relive our honeymoon.

$\mathcal{T}$hank you for trying to convince
my parents that they are not losing a son,
they're gaining a daughter.

$\mathcal{T}$hank you for calling my dad "Dad."

$\mathcal{T}$hank you for finally acquiescing
and not throwing away my aunt's wedding
gift—her hand crafted, one-of-a-kind bowl
that leaks and leans to one side.

$\mathcal{T}$hank you for pulling the bowl
from the back of the closet and putting it
on display when my aunt came to visit.

*T*hank you for promising
to inform me before you stop taking
oral contraceptives.

*T*hank you for not wanting
twelve children.

*T*hank you for nibbling on my ear
and nuzzling me in all the right places
to get me in the mood.

*T*hank you for kissing me with long,
deep, moist, passionate kisses, as if you had
all the time in the world.

*T*hank you for screaming and moaning
when I got it right.

*T*hank you for always moaning
my name during intimate moments.

*T*hank you for making me see
stars and rockets' red glare.

*T*hank you for the nights that never end
and convalescing with me the morning after.

*T*hank you for easing my fear by telling me
that your "friend" paid its monthly visit.

*T*hank you for showing me how much you love
me every second of every hour of every day.

*T*hank you for driving nowhere
special just to see what's there.

*T*hank you for putting quarters in the
jukebox and selecting my favorite songs.

*T*hank you for watching "60 Minutes"
with me every Sunday night.

*T*hank you for never doing anything bad that
would attract the attention of Ed Bradley.

*T*hank you for including me in your
wishes when you blow out candles.

*T*hank you for not throwing away my disco eight-
track tapes, Little League trophies, Cub Scouts
uniform, *Richie Rich* comic books, beer
can collection, thousands of old car parts . . .

*T*hank you for reminding me how much
you trust me before I went to a bachelor party
or out on the town with the guys.

*T*hank you for not giving me
the third degree when I got home.

*T*hank you for tickling me
in all the right places.

*T*hank you for not plucking
my chest hairs—all two of them.

*T*hank you for not coming to bed or
running to the store with curlers in your hair.

*T*hank you for running your fingers
through my thinning hair and trying
to convince me that it isn't thinning.

*T*hank you for not suggesting that I go
to Hair Club for Men or spray-paint my scalp.

*T*hank you for not telling me that bald is sexy.

$\mathcal{T}$hank you for not yakking on the phone
to your girlfriends all night long.

$\mathcal{T}$hank you for kissing me behind the knees.

$\mathcal{T}$hank you for making a surprise guest
appearance in my shower.

*T*hank you for spicing up TV dinners with
candles, red wine, and Louisiana hot sauce.

*T*hank you for taking a picture
of me with Mickey at Disneyland.

*T*hank you for trying
to curb your "moodiness" around me.

$\mathscr{T}$hank you for explaining how
your plumbing . . . *er* . . . anatomy works.

$\mathscr{T}$hank you for letting me eat
all of the lions in the Animal Crackers box.

$\mathscr{T}$hank you for not practicing
reverse psychology on me.

$\mathscr{T}$hank you for blowing kisses
to me across a crowded room.

*T*hank you for using your
frequent-flyer miles on me.

*T*hank you for inducting me
into the Mile High Club.

*T*hank you for letting the devil
make you do it every so often.

*T*hank you for not bragging to your girlfriends
about my performance in the sack.

*T*hank you for making me blush
when you read out loud the steamy passages
from trashy romance novels.

$\mathcal{T}$hank you for laughing
at those stupid guys on "Studs."

$\mathcal{T}$hank you for bringing tears to my eyes
when you say you couldn't live without me.

*T*hank you for bringing home
an armful of travel brochures so that
we can plan the perfect escape.

*T*hank you for helping me
tuck my shirttails into my pants.

$\mathscr{T}$hank you for not flirting
with other men.

$\mathscr{T}$hank you for firmly stating "I've gotta man"
when other men flirt with you.

$\mathscr{T}$hank you for preparing
tea and scones on a
quiet Sunday afternoon.

$\mathcal{T}$hank you for playing
rub-a-dub-dub in the tub.

$\mathcal{T}$hank you for being my rubber ducky
and squeaking when I squeeze you.

*T*hank you for starting a pillow fight
and letting me win sometimes.

*T*hank you for lazing in bed with me
on a Saturday morning and watching
the Coyote chase the Road Runner.

*T*hank you for helping me finally figure
out what a Venus butterfly is.

*T*hank you for still having a crush
on me after all these years.

*T*hank you for snuggling
with me in bed as we read.

*T*hank you for boosting my confidence
with your words of encouragement.

*T*hank you for cleaning
your hair from the sink drain.

*T*hank you for sending me five postcards
over five straight days with one word written
on each: Very, Love, I, Much, You.

*T*hank you for being
my personal image consultant.

*T*hank you for not comparing me to other guys
that you know, including your father.

*T*hank you for buying me a new ice cream when
my scoop fell to the ground.

*T*hank you for cherishing our love.

*T*hank you for not making me explain
why I enjoy watching Moe smack Curly.

*T*hank you for not being a sore loser
when I beat you at strip checkers.

*T*hank you for greeting me at the front door
wearing a red teddy and a smile.

*T*hank you for letting me watch you undress.

*T*hank you for not accusing me of having
only one thing on my mind!

$\mathcal{T}$hank you for not listening to the
tick-tock of your biological clock.

$\mathcal{T}$hank you for eating the charred mystery dinner
that I cooked for you while keeping a smile on your
face no matter how awful it tasted.

$\mathcal{T}$hank you for not letting
a broken fingernail ruin your day.

*T*hank you for buying the pump
dispenser after I kept forgetting
to put the cap on the toothpaste.

*T*hank you for not making me
feel inadequate around cucumbers.

*T*hank you for not lying to me.

*T*hank you for starring in my daydreams.

$\mathcal{T}$hank you for keeping our secrets secret.

$\mathcal{T}$hank you for not letting
us become a divorce statistic.

$\mathcal{T}$hank you for promising to meet me
in the afterlife so that we can spend
an eternity together—even if you come back
as a cat and I come back as a dog.

$\mathscr{T}$hank you for warming my side
of the bed before I get in.

$\mathscr{T}$hank you for telling me about
your day and asking about mine.

Thank you for not disturbing me as I sit
on my throne with my newspaper.

Thank you for replacing the empty roll of toilet
paper and not leaving me stranded.

Thank you for showing me that bathrooms
can smell pleasant with potpourri.

*T*hank you for writing a list of 99
original reasons why I'm special and
taking it to a copy center to have it
bound just in time for my birthday.

*T*hank you for doing new things
to your hair even when I didn't notice.

*T*hank you for not running away with
your friends Thelma and Louise.

*T*hank you for feeding me the best-tasting
fiber you can find to keep me regular.

*T*hank you for finding bargains at the outlets.

*T*hank you for not telling me
"I told you so" when I deserve it.

*T*hank you for leaving
my holey socks and underwear alone.

*T*hank you for screening
your calls and always taking mine.

*T*hank you for not wearing so much perfume
that it lingers over you like a storm cloud.

$\mathscr{T}$hank you for kissing me every morning when we wake up despite my morning breath.

$\mathscr{T}$hank you for writing sexy messages in my date book telling me where I had to be and when and what to wear and what you're going to do to me.

$\mathscr{T}$hank you for all of our tender moments.

*T*hank you for every so often greeting
me as I step from the shower
with a towel warmed by the dryer.

*T*hank you for picking up my pile of clothes that
don't make it to the hamper.

*T*hank you for telling me the dirty jokes
you hear at the office.

*T*hank you for letting me use your
moisturizer to soothe my razor burn.

*T*hank you for not being
an authority on every subject.

*T*hank you for not holding it against me
that I don't have Rambo's buns.

*T*hank you for not bashing
my "species" too hard.

*T*hank you for curling up on the sofa with
me to watch old Clint Eastwood movies.

*T*hank you for running errands for me,
like picking up my shirts, returning my
videos, shopping for my mom's birthday gifts.

*T*hank you for telling me that I'm
the sexiest man alive despite my love handles.

*T*hank you for using your hair spray sparingly so
that I can light a match in your presence.

*T*hank you for being a great
Dr. Mom by kissing my boo-boos.

*T*hank you for watching out
for my best interests.

*T*hank you for not throwing
breakable objects (or any objects) at me.

*T*hank you for getting on the other
phone extension, asking for my credit
card number, and playing 1-900 with me.

*T*hank you for pulling
most of the weight around the house.

*T*hank you for not making me
carry your purse in public.

*T*hank you for completing
my thoughts and . . .

$\mathcal{T}$hank you for not reminding me about my exercise equipment that is crammed in the back of the closet.

$\mathcal{T}$hank you for keeping track of impending special dates like anniversaries and birthdays so that I don't forget.

*T*hank you for playing sex kitten
every once in a while. *Meow . . .*

*T*hank you for saying how much you loved the
gifts that I picked out by myself, even the outfits that
you wouldn't be caught dead in.

*T*hank you for not trying on every dress in
the store before deciding which one to buy.

*T*hank you for not using the shower rod as a clothesline for your panty hose and lingerie.

*T*hank you for buying me flowers from street vendors, even though they're really for you.

*T*hank you for listening to me no matter how hard it gets at times.

$\mathscr{T}$hank you for not wearing high heels
that make you tower over me.

$\mathscr{T}$hank you for living up to
your promise when you say, "Honest,
you can tell me, I won't get mad."

$\mathscr{T}$hank you for letting me play in The Sharper
Image while you shop in the rest of the mall.

*T*hank you for not having your old
boyfriend's name tattooed on your butt.

*T*hank you for redefining beauty
and chic in all that you do.

*T*hank you for not spending
all of Saturday at the beauty salon.

*T*hank you for not making me come out
of hiding when you throw a baby shower
for your friend in our living room.

*T*hank you for not coming out of hiding
when I have the boys over to play poker,
so we can smoke cigars and swear.

$\mathscr{T}$hank you for cheering me on
at my softball games.

$\mathscr{T}$hank you for making my favorite appetizer,
Cheez Whiz® spread on crackers, before my favorite
dinner, cocktail wienies and beer.

$\mathscr{T}$hank you for letting the phone ring when
we're rolling between red satin sheets.

$\mathscr{T}$hank you for forbidden pleasures
like a *ménage à trois* with you,
me, and Mr. Bubble.

$\mathscr{T}$hank you for not criticizing me in public.

$\mathscr{T}$hank you for reassuring
me when I'm in doubt.

$\mathscr{T}$hank you for being civil to my frat brothers
when they visited us for a three-day weekend.

$\mathscr{T}$hank you for beating the national average by
making love more than 1.3 times per week.

$\mathscr{T}$hank you for fighting fair
and not hitting below the belt.

$\mathscr{T}$hank you for returning home to me a
little calmer after storming out in anger.

$\mathscr{T}$hank you for not recycling lame excuses
like "It was on sale" or "I have a headache."

*T*hank you for being my steady Saturday
night date until death do us part.

*T*hank you for being a tourist with me
and exploring new cities by foot.

*T*hank you for not saying
"you don't understand me" *too often*.

$\mathcal{T}$hank you for making a roast with
all the trimmings as a surprise
when you came home from work early.

$\mathcal{T}$hank you for being my dessert.

*T*hank you for shoving me in the right direction
when I needed it most.

*T*hank you for reading *How to
Make Love to a Man* and practicing on me.

*T*hank you for bowling with me
and not laughing at my gutter balls.

*T*hank you for giving me
the benefit of the doubt when you
didn't know my Scrabble® game words.

*T*hank you for waiting in a long line
with me at the movie theater for an Arnold
movie that you didn't want to see.

*T*hank you for our afternoon delights.

*T*hank you for not calling me names that hurt.

*T*hank you for not letting your cold feet touch my
warm body when you jump into bed.

*T*hank you for clipping cartoons from the
newspapers for me to enjoy.

*T*hank you for being my security blanket.

*T*hank you for not taking away my other security blanket—the remote control.

*T*hank you for living with my "little" idiosyncrasies, like my urge to zap 62 TV channels in 22 seconds flat.

*T*hank you for teaching me
how to count calories and fat grams.

*T*hank you for letting your imagination
run wild when we make love.

*T*hank you for brushing the white specks and
lint balls from my suits before I leave for work.

*T*hank you for not letting your daily
horoscope influence your moods.

*T*hank you for replying "Now there's more
for me to love" when I complain about
the ten extra pounds I've gained over the years.

*T*hank you for leaving purple and red hickeys on
places that I can cover up for work the next day.

*T*hank you for stopping me
from worrying too much.

*T*hank you for offering me
a breath mint when I needed one.

*T*hank you for not draping your arm around
me in public like a "No Trespassing" sign.

$\mathcal{T}$hank you for taking me away for
some R&R and TLC at a little B&B.

$\mathcal{T}$hank you for not playing tit for tat with me.

$\mathcal{T}$hank you for not ordering anchovies
on the pizza because you'll taste fishy.

$\mathcal{T}$hank you for sharing
everything with me, even the flu.

*T*hank you for not reading
Playgirl to see how I stack up.

*T*hank you for finding my contact lens when
I thought it dropped down the drain.

*T*hank you for getting me out of that speeding
ticket when you convinced the police officer that
you were pregnant and you had to pee *NOW!!!*

*T*hank you for encouraging me to wear
my silk boxer shorts around the house.

*T*hank you for not requesting
that I shave on weekends.

*T*hank you for growing to love my parents
and thinking of them as our good friends.

*T*hank you for going to my reunion
and not remarking about the effects
of gravity on my former girlfriends.

*T*hank you for wanting to live
with me until 100 so that Willard Scott
will announce our birthdays.

*T*hank you for telling me when
I'm wearing two different colored socks.

*T*hank you for suggesting
a test run of the *Kama Sutra.*

*T*hank you for giving
to charities that protect baby seals.

$\mathcal{T}$hank you for always striving
to do your best.

$\mathcal{T}$hank you for not dressing like Cher
at an Oscar night.

$\mathcal{T}$hank you for letting me drive your car—
all the time!

$\mathcal{T}$hank you for not being a backseat driver.

*T*hank you for replying, "Infinity divided by one over infinity all to the infinite power," when I ask you, "How much do you love me?"

*T*hank you for introducing me to the incredibly
smooth voice of Nat King Cole.

*T*hank you for letting me
have the window seat on the plane.

*T*hank you for taking me
to the aquarium and pointing out the fish
that look and pucker like me.

Thank you for teaching me to care
about things that are important to you.

Thank you for not applying
your makeup while you're driving.

Thank you for playing couch potato
with me in front of the TV
on a Friday night after a tough week.

*T*hank you for never telling
me the honeymoon's over.

*T*hank you for letting me
cry on your shoulders.

*T*hank you for not making me buy
your tampons in a crowded Quik-e-Mart.

*T*hank you for finding
the best gifts for my parents.

*T*hank you for only eating garlic
and onions when we both do.

*T*hank you for not getting *too* jealous
when I speak to another woman.

*T*hank you for massaging my aching muscles
after a workout on the tennis court.

*T*hank you for teaching me patience.

*T*hank you for not kicking me
out of bed for eating crackers.

*T*hank you for sharing with me the kind of
love that makes other people envious.

$\mathscr{T}$hank you for insisting that you wouldn't sleep
with Robert Redford for a million bucks.

$\mathscr{T}$hank you for putting
romance back in my life.

$\mathscr{T}$hank you for always calling me
when you are going to be late.

$\mathcal{T}$hank you for framing photos of us
and placing them around the house
so that I can always look at you.

$\mathcal{T}$hank you for forgiving me
when I have hurt you.

Thank you for explaining why whites come
out pink when washed with new reds.

Thank you for finding my socks
that the washing machine ate.

Thank you for taking my clothes out of
my bureau and refolding them for me.

Thank you for picking up
where my mom left off.

*T*hank you for not leering at other guys while in my presence—especially Chippendale dancers on "Donahue" or that Fabio character on the covers of romance novels.

*T*hank you for not tickling me when you play with my love handles.

*T*hank you for giving me that special
medicine called "love" that no doctor
could prescribe and no pharmacist could
bottle, label, and mark up the price of.

*T*hank you for not answering
"I dunno, what do you want to do?"
every time I ask "What do you wanna do?"

*T*hank you for not singing "Rise and shine!"
in my ear at 6 A.M. on our days off.

*T*hank you for not being
too competitive with me.

*T*hank you for sharing *The Joy of Sex* with me.

*T*hank you for disclosing
your hidden agendas.

*T*hank you for being there at the end of
"one of those days" and reminding me of
all the good things we have, like our health,
our family, our love, each other.

*T*hank you for being a trouper
and going to the store to buy condoms.

*T*hank you for juggling all that you do.

*T*hank you for having
realistic expectations of me.

*T*hank you for keeping me young.

*T*hank you for not
threatening me with ". . . or else!"

*T*hank you for your woman's intuition.

*T*hank you for keeping the lights on
so that we can look into each other's
eyes when we make love.

*T*hank you for indulging the boy in me with
uninterrupted playtime on Nintendo®.

*T*hank you for taking the blame
to help me save face.

*T*hank you for tossing a Frisbee
with me and my dog.

*T*hank you for swinging with me—
on a schoolyard swing set, that is!

*T*hank you for spending
your pay raises on me.

*T*hank you for seducing me
in the back of a limo.

*T*hank you for not acting like Roseanne
Conner, Peg Bundy, or Rebecca Howe.

$\mathscr{T}$hank you for not disclosing the office gossip
that I share with you and getting me in trouble
when you meet my friends from work.

$\mathscr{T}$hank you for not whining like Daddy's little girl
and pouting when you don't get your way.

$\mathscr{T}$hank you for letting me blast
the air conditioner to get the room
temperature down to 50 degrees.

$\mathcal{T}$hank you for my special nicknames.

$\mathcal{T}$hank you for not calling me
by my special nicknames in public.

*T*hank you for not scheduling
appointments for us to make love.

*T*hank you for investing in our relationship by
doing those quizzes in the women's magazines.

*T*hank you for not believing
the answers to those quizzes that say
you need to find a new lover.

*T*hank you for not holding a grudge
against me for the rest of my life
and plotting ways to get even with me.

*T*hank you for helping me
with crossword puzzles.

*T*hank you for letting me have
the last word every once in a while.

*T*hank you for not embarrassing me by imitating
Meg Ryan in the *When Harry Met Sally* restaurant
scene when we are in public.

*T*hank you for reminding me to slow down when
you see that I get overwhelmed with stress.

*T*hank you for reading my mind.

*T*hank you for never going to bed mad
at me or banishing me to the couch.

Thank you for checking my body for ticks
after romps in the woods.

Thank you for not expecting me to be perfect.

Thank you for my Odor-Eaters.

Thank you for patting me on the back
for a job well done.

*T*hank you for wearing fish-net stockings
and stiletto heels—just once.

*T*hank you for letting me
use your toothbrush.

*T*hank you for adding to my
collection of power tools.

*T*hank you for leaving my power tools alone.

$\mathcal{T}$hank you for not patronizing me.

$\mathcal{T}$hank you for not using
Madonna as your role model.

$\mathcal{T}$hank you for buying me
new socks to replace the old ones
that keep falling down around my ankles.

$\mathcal{T}$hank you for saving a little bit of room
in the bedroom closet for me.

 $\mathcal{T}$hank you for letting me
pick from your dinner plate.

 $\mathcal{T}$hank you for telling me when
I've had too much to drink.

 $\mathcal{T}$hank you for stopping along the highway
so that I can pee in the bushes.

$\mathscr{T}$hank you for not using all of
the hot water during your showers or
flushing the toilet when I'm in the shower.

$\mathscr{T}$hank you for understanding that I'm unable to
be romantic every day—but I'm trying!!!

$\mathscr{T}$hank you for not breaking my heart.

*T*hank you for believing me
when I say, "I'm sorry."

*T*hank you for always being in my corner
and urging me on between the rounds.

*T*hank you for dazzling me.

*T*hank you for sharing your dreams with me.

*T*hank you for exploring new worlds with me.

*T*hank you for being my hero.

*T*hank you for making me laugh.

*T*hank you for vowing to love me
until the end of time.

*T*hank you for your faith in me.

*T*hank you for being the perfect mate in this life,
as well as in prior and future lives.

*T*hank you for making me your number-one
priority.

*T*hank you for not raining on my parades.

*T*hank you for sharing the good, the bad,
and even the ugly with me.

*T*hank you for filling my emotional needs.

*T*hank you for being my *bestest* friend
in the whole wide world.

*T*hank you for making a commitment to us.

*T*hank you for taking care of me.

*T*hank you for the daily dose of joy and
laughter that you bring into my life.

*T*hank you for your kindness and compassion.

*T*hank you for telling me that
"I'd like a son just like you."

*T*hank you for being my number-one fan.

*T*hank you for smiling—a lot.

*T*hank you for accepting me for who I am.

*T*hank you for waiting all of your life for me.

*T*hank you for starting our own traditions.

*T*hank you for telling me that
time began when you met me.

*T*hank you for being you.

$\mathcal{T}$hank you for being mine—
always and forever.

SPECIAL THANK-YOUS JUST FOR THE WOMAN I LOVE

Thank you _____

_____

Thank you _____

_____

Thank you _____

_____

Thank you _____

_____

About the Authors

Scott Matthews and Tamara Nikuradse are married and live with their three cats, Black Beauty, Lisa, and Dog Meat.

The happy couple is expecting a puppy any day now.

After *Dear Mom, Thank You for Being Mine* and *Dear Dad, Thank You for Being Mine* were published, we received many original thank-yous that people wrote for their parents, and we enjoyed reading them. If you have a special thank-you for the man or woman you love that you'd like to share, please send it to:

SCOTT MATTHEWS AND TAMARA NIKURADSE
c/o BALLANTINE BOOKS
201 EAST 50TH STREET
NEW YORK, NY 10022

Please include your name and address so that we can give you credit if we use your thank-yous in future editions.
Thank you.

DON'T FORGET THE MAN YOU LOVE!

- Thank you for asking me for a date instead of hitting me over the head with your club and dragging me by my hair back to your cave.
- Thank you for not considering dinner on our first date as foreplay.
- Thank you for not expecting a reward like a barking seal every time you perform a chore.
- Thank you for not zapping the channels with the remote (hint . . . hint . . .).
- Thank you for sending a card to my mother on Mother's Day thanking her for creating me.

To the Man I Love, Thank You for Being Mine—
ask for it at your favorite bookstore.